CHELTENHAM CARAVANS: AN ILLUSTRATED HISTORY

JACQUI MCCARTHY

AMBERLEY

First published 2017

Amberley Publishing
The Hill, Stroud,
Gloucestershire, GL5 4EP

www.amberley-books.com

Map illustration by Thomas Bohm, User Design, Illustration and Typesetting.

ISBN: 978 1 4456 6516 0 (print)
ISBN: 978 1 4456 6517 7 (ebook)

British Library Cataloguing in Publication Data.
A catalogue record for this book is available from the British Library.

Typeset in 10pt on 13pt Celeste.
Origination by Amberley Publishing.
Printed in the UK.

Contents

What makes a Cheltenham caravan special? It is certainly a combination of innovative design and expert engineering along with the dedication and determination of one man and his family to produce a van of excellent quality and style at a fair price. The Cheltenham caravans still in use today are testament to their success.

A 1960s Sable.

Beginning

Mr Arthur Gardner built a motor caravan *c.* 1920. After intensive testing, he decided that a trailer caravan would be a more practical option and set about designing and constructing his first caravan. After securing some stables at his home to use as a workplace, the process began.

Once the caravan had been built, Mr Gardner and a friend took it on an extensive trip around the country in order to test it thoroughly. The outing was a great success and on his return he set about implementing the small changes needed to enhance it even further. After completing the improvements, and satisfied he had created a quality van, Mr Gardner went on to build more vans – always endeavouring to improve on the last one.

1924

By 1924, Mr Gardner had moved production from the Farm to the Maida Vale Works, Cheltenham. At this time the company was still named Summerfield Caravans. In the first year at Cheltenham, three caravans were produced as a hire fleet. Over the next few years the fleet expanded and a number of customers who had hired the vans enjoyed the experience so much that they then expressed a keen interest in owning their own van. Mr Gardner soon realised if he didn't start to manufacture the caravans to sell to his customers, they would seek to purchase one from an alternative company. With this in mind the 'Cheltenham Caravan Company' was formed and vans were now produced for purchase.

1926

In 1926, Arthur Gardner married his friend's daughter Joyce (known as Joy). Over the years, Joy had shown a lot of interest in the vans. She had regularly accompanied her father on his many visits to assist Arthur in the design, building, and testing of the vans. Once married, Joy took on responsibility of sales. This was quite a challenge as, once the decision to sell the vans had been taken, production increased dramatically, so it was vital that buyers were found. The vans soon gained a reputation for excellent quality and strength, which helped to secure sales, and they managed to sell every van produced.

Joy gave a female perspective to the design and usability of the layout, as well as choosing the soft furnishings and carpets in order to create the right ambience for those hiring the vans, or for purchasers that bought the vans fitted out.

Car ownership was still a privilege of the wealthy and when customers came to purchase a caravan very few had a coupling fitted, so this became an added service that the Cheltenham Caravan Company provided.

1929

By 1929 the company was producing caravan bodies in varying sizes and finishes. There was a domed roof model in three sizes and a clerestory model (lantern roof) in three sizes. These could be bought unfurnished or fitted out with beds, cookers, and so on.

A 1929 Domed Roof Caravan.

A 1929 Clestory Caravan.

Prices of vans, with clestory and fitted with chest of drawers, are :—

	Painted ply	Canvas covered ply	Steel faced ply	Aluminium faced ply
8ft × 6ft 4ins to sleep three. Single burner stove and accessories ...	£100	£105 0 0	£110 0 0	£115 0 0
10ft × 6ft 4ins to sleep four, including double burner cooker and accessories	£115	£120 0 0	£127 0 0	£135 0 0
12ft × 6ft 4ins to sleep four with division & all accessories	£135	£140 0 0	£147 10 0	£155 0 0

Bay window, if required, £2 2s. 0d. extra.

	Painted Ply	Ply covered with canvas	Steel faced Ply	Aluminium faced ply
8ft × 6ft to sleep three. Single burner cooker and equipment	£85	£90 0 0	£92 10 0	£97 10 0
10ft × 6ft 4ins to sleep four. Double burner cooker, and equipment ...	£100	£107 10 0	£112 10 0	£117 10 0
12ft × 6ft 4ins to sleep four including accessories & partition	£125	£132 10 0	£137 10 0	£145 0 0

Any of above may be fitted with bay window at an extra cost of £2 2s. 0d.

5

1929 Price List for Domed Roof Caravans.

The Chassis consisted of two channel steel runners of a substantial cross section. The springs, underslung, were fixed to the channel with hardened shackle bolts fitted with greasers. The wheels had 27 x 4.40 cord tyres which were interchangeable with a Morris wheel. The brakes were internal expanding brakes and automatically came on if the van were to overrun the car. The draw bar had two phosphor bronze bearings, which carried the sliding shaft. This took the pull, through a suitable coil spring, and operated the brakes. Another lighter spring stopped the buffering action. The coupling consisted of a ball and socket, designed by Mr Gardner. This was the first ball-headed pin – a one and a half inch with six start thread – which stopped the chattering that happened with a straight-pin coupling. The corner steadies were a fold-up design; the ones at the rear folded up with the step. Sockets were fitted at the front and rear of the van, making it easier to attach to the car wherever it was parked. When travelling at night the car was connected to the front socket and the rear lamp to the back one.

The caravan bodies were constructed on an ash frame with plywood panelling. They offered three different levels of finish. The first was a covering of canvas which was stuck down and covered with white lead. The next option was thin sheet-steel cemented on top of plywood. The better option was aluminium, which is lighter, stronger, and non-corrosive. The aluminium model could be left polished. The vans were painted cream with chocolate mouldings, although they could be finished in any colour desired. All models could be fitted with a bay window at an extra cost of £2 2s.

Internally, the ceilings were white enamelled and the wall panels finished in a light-coloured stain to help preserve the light and give a spacious feel. A dark Jacobean stain could be used if requested. Electric lights were standard on all vans; the twelve-foot models had two lamps fitted. There was a partition that could be put across the van, dividing it into two areas – one side housing the double bed and the other two singles – and this could be purchased at extra cost. In the better models was a chest of drawers which incorporated a washbowl fitted with a waste pipe. The vans came with a Valor 'Perfection' cooker, including oven unless a different one was desired. In the domed roof models the settees pulled out to form the beds, and the third bed hinged up across the foot of the other beds at the front of the van. Included in the price of the vans was a range of equipment – *see below*.

Equipment supplied with all caravans and included in the list prices :—

Cups and saucers	Baking tin	Pepper, salt, mustard
Egg cups	Pie dish	Knives
Large plates	Saucepans	Forks
Small ,,	Kettle	Tea spoons
Dish	Bucket	Dessert ,,
Fruit bowls	Frying pan	Table ,,
Glasses	Wash bowl	Can opener
Jugs	Valor Perfection	Plug and flexible lead
Teapot	stove and oven	for lighting.

An equipment list from 1929.

The vans were still available for hire and prices varied depending on the size of van and the season. Insurance was to be taken out by the hirer with the same company that insured the vehicle. For those that worried about towing, the brochure stated that a 10-foot van had been towed sixty-four miles in two and a half hours with a comparatively old (1924) ten point nine Clyno.

Hire charges for vans, including full equipment :

PER WEEK

	Oct.-April	May-June	July-Sept.	August.
8ft van with domed roof	£2 0 0	£3 5 0	£3 10 0	£4 0 0
do. saloon type ...	£2 10 0	£3 15 0	£4 0 0	£4 10 0
10ft, domed roof ...	£2 10 0	£3 15 0	£4 0 0	£4 10 0
do. saloon type ...	£2 15 0	£4 10 0	£5 0 0	£5 10 0
12ft van	£3 0 0	£5 0 0	£5 15 0	£6 10 0

Add £1 for fitting towing bracket, number plate, electric light lead, etc., unless the booking is for more than two weeks.

The following extra equipment is available :—

per week.		per week.	
Lean-to tent ...	10/–	Camp bed ...	2/–
Ground sheet ...	2/–	Folding table ...	2/–
Folding armchair	1/–	Extra set of crockery	1/–
Camp chair ...	6d.	Primus stove ...	1/3
Lavatory tent ...	3/6	Cushions & pillows	9d.

1930s

One of the challenges of the 1930s was how to improve the towing stability of the vans. This was a problem that Mr Gardner knew required immense skill and application. Using his knowledge and expertise he came up with a variety of solutions, of which lowering the floor was seen as the best and most effective design. This was put in place alongside other changes, which would also help. The changes included: mounting the floor below the main joists, changing from a straight axle to a cranked axle – which was pioneered by Mr Gardner – and changing the springs so they would now be sited below the axle.

Not only did these changes improve the towing stability, but they also resulted in the driver being able to have a good view straight through the van from the towing vehicle's rear-view mirror. The combination of these alterations made towing much easier and safer. In a very short time Cheltenham Caravans gained a good reputation for the excellent stability of the vans on the road.

CHASSIS

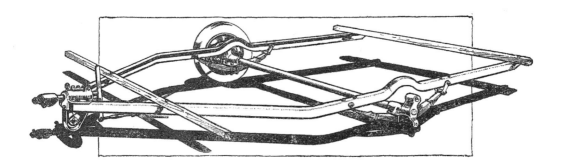

Diagram showing 1930s Cheltenham chassis.

1933

Up until 1933, Cheltenham's were sold mainly by word of mouth by satisfied customers spreading the word. After attending the RAC rally in 1933, they decided to employ the help of sales agents to promote and sell the caravans; this would enable their reputation to spread wider and quicker than at present. They also offered caravans for sale at the British Industries Fair at Castle Bromwich. This resulted in a much-improved order book, which put pressure on the company. The demand was so high that they had to implement evening shifts to try to complete the orders on time. They still struggled to keep up with demand, which meant that customers had to wait much longer for the delivery of their new caravan. The company apologised and asked that orders were placed earlier to avoid disappointment in the future.

1934 Cheltenham caravan displayed at the Owners Club 60th anniversary rally.

Interior of 1934 Cheltenham Caravan with Cheltenham pottery.

As it was still rare for cars to have a tow-bar fitted, the company continued to fit them at a cost of £1. Cecil Gardner states that this was carried on until the mid- to late 1930s, when cars started to have semi-monocoque construction, which meant the job of fitting the tow-bar required accessing the engine mounting in order to gain a solid fixing. After this they reassessed the pricing.

Around 1933–34, Mr and Mrs Gardner delivered a caravan to a diplomat in Rabat, Morocco. Before embarking on the journey they were told that supply of petrol could be a problem. The caravan had a metal bath, seated in rubber, under the offside front bed. They filled the bath with petrol at Ceuta, before taking a boat to cross the Straits of Gibraltar. These docks had only a very large rope net to lift the car and caravan on to the deck, unlike at Dover, which had a large platform you drove on to hoist you aboard. As the basket rose the caravan tipped substantially and they were frightened that the petrol would pour out. After travelling on the other side and needing to refuel, they were almost knocked out by the fumes in the van. After recovering, they found that the petrol had eaten away all the rubber and the bath had gone along with the petrol.

Interior of 1934 Cheltenham
Caravan showing the heater.

The Gardners continued to test the vans by using them extensively in the UK and abroad, always looking at ways to develop the quality and design of each model. The testing of the vans was often viewed by the family as something of a marathon, with Mr Gardner insisting on towing 100 miles before breakfast, thus avoiding the main traffic and the heat of the day. After breakfast, another 100 miles would be covered before stopping for a light lunch and an hour's rest by the roadside. It was on one of these lunch stops that Mrs Gardner had a close shave with a passing car. After this, it was decided that fitting two doors on each van – one on each side – would make them much safer when travelling abroad. This was implemented on as many models as possible. During the travelling, the vans would be towed as fast as safety would allow, in order to test them thoroughly. Much later, when Cecil Gardner and his family took over the testing, they did not start quite so early and yet still managed to cover on average 225 miles a day, which is still quite an achievement with two small children on board.

1936

At the Caravan Club's first National Rally, which took place in Leamington Spa in 1936, a Cheltenham Caravan created a great deal of interest. Major Presland (London Caravan Company Ltd) had taken along his newly purchased Cheltenham van, which had liquid petroleum gas cooking, lighting, and hot water radiators. The innovative lantern roof was also greatly admired, not only for providing extra headroom and bringing a light and airy feel internally to the van, but for the excellent design, which was aerodynamic and added to the style and elegance. This reinforced that Cheltenham caravans were leading the way in new designs and innovations.

The Gardners used paraffin fuelled fridges in the vans before the war. They would light it at Cheltenham and keep it lit until they arrived back home. It did cause them concerns, especially with the paraffin being sloshed around going over bumps and when stopping. These fridges were only used by the family and were never fitted into any of the other vans because of the safety issue. After the war, butane fridges were fitted.

1937

Metal windows were introduced this year and as always they were of high quality, being made of chromium-plated brass so they would remain rust free. Panelling on the vans was changed to synthetic material, instead of three-ply wood, and this made them more resistant to the cold and damp. The roof consisted of insulation board covered with cloth, which was made watertight. It resisted heat, which allowed the van to stay cool in the sunshine and also ensured that through the winter there was no condensation.

The models this year included a Super Deluxe van which had a semi-circular toilet compartment door, a dressing table with swing mirrors, and a bath under one of the bunks. Calor Gas was used for the cooking, lighting, heating the water for the bath and for the radiator system. The pipes for the system ran through the wardrobe and the clothes lockers. A storage battery powered the electric lights. It was described in the brochure as 'Truly a Palace on Wheels'.

1937 – 37P three-berth model.

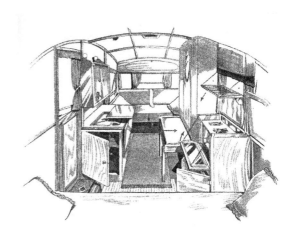

THE CHELTENHAM MODEL 37·P
THREE BERTH

Interior length	...	11 ft. 3 in.
Interior width	...	6 ft. 3 in.
Head room	...	6 ft. 2 in.
Overall height	...	7 ft. 7 in.

1937 – 37P interior.

1937 – 57SD Super Deluxe model.

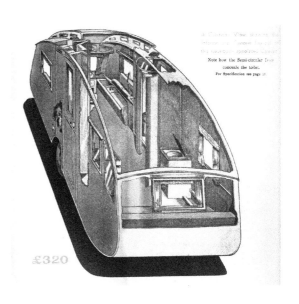

1937 – 67SD Super Deluxe model showing the bath under front bed.

15

The Gardners took a van to the FICC Rally in Wiesbaden, Germany. This was to prove a most adventurous trip. While there, they went to view the *Graf Zeppelin* and, after losing their way on the return journey, ended up close to a military base where they were very nearly arrested. They also thought it very strange that butter and other luxury groceries were only available to foreigners and were kept under the counter; on later reflection they realised this was all part of the preparation for the forthcoming war. The caravan fascinated the local children, who, one night, climbed onto the roof and peeped through the lights to see what was happening inside this strange van – a very amusing experience for everyone.

1938

After years of continuing high demand for the caravans and the 'Holidays with Pay Act' coming into force, The Cheltenham Caravan Company acquired additional premises at 205 Leckhampton Road, Cheltenham and started using modern machines, making them more efficient and productive. This enabled them to build up a stock of parts, furniture, moulds and so on, over the wintertime. Once the orders started arriving, around early spring, the vans could be assembled more quickly than previously, therefore minimising the number of late deliveries.

After a suggestion from a South African customer, the models were given names instead of numbers and letters. In came The Reindeer, The Gazelle, The Antelope, The Stag, The Moose and The Eland; gone were the 47P, 67SD etc.

The pre-war Eland was described in a brochure as

Magnificence. Designed, built and equipped for all the year round use: extra-sturdy, large and lavishly appointed. Emphatically a home in any weather – a luxury flat on wheels.

The front of the 1938 Cheltenham Sales brochure.

A. China cabinet.
B. Sideboard, large larder under.
C. Washbowl.
D. Stoves.
E. Single bed, folds up by day.
F. Portable table.
G. Single bed.
H. Chest of drawers.
I. Large wardrobe.
J. Double bed.

PLAN OF ANTELOPE

£149
Double Panelled
£15 extra

1938 four-berth
Antelope,
showing
floorplan.

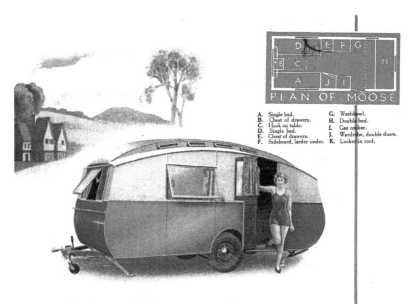

PLAN OF MOOSE

A. Single bed.
B. Chest of drawers.
C. Hook on table.
D. Single bed.
E. Chest of drawers.
F. Sideboard, larder under.
G. Washbowl.
H. Double bed.
I. Gas cooker.
J. Wardrobe, double doors.
K. Locker in roof.

£195
Without gas, complete with oil cooker £12 less.
Wireless £9 extra.

1938 four-berth
Moose,
showing
floorplan.

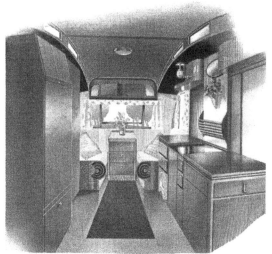

£175
Without Gas, but
complete with
oil cookers,
£12 less

A and B 4 ft. settees
C Chest of drawers
D Ventilated larder
E Drawers
F Wash bowl
G Two lockers for GasCylinders
H Double bed-settee
I Wardrobe
J Gas cooker
K Rack for papers

PLAN OF STAG

Above left: 1938 Moose interior towards front.

Above right: 1938 Four-berth Stag.

1938 interior of the Stag cooking area.

It cost £265, had triple insulation in the walls, and a double protection roof. It also had a gas fire, gas heater, gas cooker and a hot and cold water system. The water system consisted of a 16-gallon water tank under the floor and a 4-gallon tank on top of the cupboard, which was heated by gas. This fed the metal bath, which was positioned under one of the beds at the front of the van, as well as the wash basin. A chrome tap inside the cupboard operated a semi-rotary pump that directed the water where needed. On the door of the cupboard was a tip-up wash bowl, a towel rail, a glass, and a soap dish. When the cupboard and the wardrobe door were open they met and formed a partition, creating two separate rooms – each having its own fire, water supply, and door. The rear section was the chauffeur's compartment. There was a sliding panel in the division so the chauffeur could pass tea, for example, through to his employers. Cecil Gardner still recalls at least two customers who used it this way. The beds in the centre of the van could be made as a double or two singles with a walkway between. One of the beds could be taken out of the van completely and

Right: 1938 Four-berth Eland, note the two doors on the same side.

Below: 1938 Eland floorplan.

£ 2 6 5
with Hot and Cold
Cupboard

A. Single bed.
B. Drop end.
C. Chest of drawers.
D. Single bed.
E. Bath under.
F. Drop end of **D**.
G. H. & C. water system.
H. Single bed.

I. Single bed, slides under **H**.
J. Large wardrobe.
K. Small wardrobe.
L. Elsan compartment.
M. Gas cooker.
N. Wash basin.
O. Rubbish bin.
P. Sideboard, folding top.
Q. Hook on table.

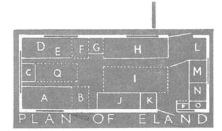

1938 Eland interior.

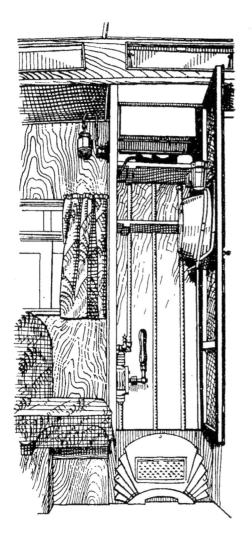

Diagram of 1938 Eland water system.

The Cheltenham stand at the 1938 Motor Show.

Cheltenham

welcome you to

Stand 52

to see

THE FINEST RANGE OF MODELS EVER SHOWN ON ONE STAND

BE SURE TO SEE THE GNU MODEL

Cheltenham take a great step forward with this entirely new 16 ft. model. It is metal panelled but yet has a lantern roof. Three rooms, end kitchen, 2 wash bowls, car type drop windows, toilet room; these are some of the features you get and all for **£250**

OTHER EXHIBITS ARE
The " ELAND " **£275**
The " STAG " **£175**
The "REINDEER" **£115**
The " GAZELLE "
which has been re-designed with a door dividing the Caravan into 2 rooms. Price **£110**

**MAIDA VALE WORKS
NAUNTON LANE
CHELTENHAM**
Telephone : 3572

CHELTENHAM
CARAVAN
COMPANY LTD

HITCH YOUR CAR
TO A CHELTENHAM

**205, LECKHAMPTON RD
CHELTENHAM**
Telephone : 3535

1938 Motor Show – Cheltenham stand information.

be used elsewhere as a camp bed. The van also had two wardrobes, a Parkinson stove, a ventilated food safe, a Bakelite sideboard, a china cupboard, a cocktail cabinet, an 'Invicta' wireless set, a paper rack, and flower vases. This year's sales brochure acknowledges Joy's input in the caravan design. Under 'The Kitchen' heading, in points to remember, it states, 'Cheltenham caravan kitchens are planned by a practical woman caravanner of long experience. Completely efficient, they give the greatest working ease.'

The Cheltenham Caravan Company showcased the 1939 models – which were, according to them, 'The finest range of models ever shown on one stand' – at the motor show at Olympia in London. The show started 14 October 1938.

The Eland, £275, was shown as the improved version, now having a bay window and two doors. This was also to be the last year of the Fawn, although the name was revived in 1964.

The Gnu, £250, was the main attraction. It had been part of the ongoing development programme and was intended to replace the Moose. It had an all-steel body and a lantern roof. Unfortunately, this was to prove very difficult to build and was not popular with the buyers; therefore, not a viable option for the company. Production ceased quite quickly and did not begin again after the war. Part of the problem could be that at the time Coventry Steel Caravans had already made an impact on this market.

All caravans came with a full set of crockery, which was manufactured by Palissy in Stoke-on-Trent.

1938 Cheltenham stand review by *The Caravan* magazine.

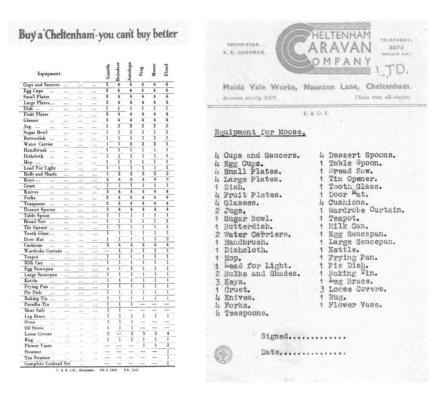

Above left: List of equipment included in the purchase of the vans in 1938.

Above right: 1938 docket of equipment to be purchased with a Moose caravan.

1939

The Eland had further improvements made which included a new layout and having only one door on each side.

This year Smith Instruments of Cricklewood built a shadow factory near the Cheltenham works. Their advance staff used Cheltenham caravans to live in. The Cheltenham Company built 'Evacuation' models for them to use – these were a Moose model, but with much better insulation and a solid-fuel stove. Only three were built, as not long afterwards all the able men left for the forces, with the remaining staff building farm-fuel trailers for the Ministry of Agriculture. The rest of the factory at Maida Vale was used for storage of government materials. The Antelope factory at Leckhampton was used for aircraft production.

Although caravan production stopped during the war, caravans proved to be very practical and were used by various organisations as mobile bases and offices, including air raid warden bases and canteens. People lived in caravans throughout the war for a variety of reasons; some viewing this as a safer option than staying in their own homes, some after their homes had been destroyed, and some as evacuees. At this time, most vans were built for summer use and didn't have a great deal of insulation; they were extremely cold throughout the winter, unless you were lucky enough to have the skills and materials to make the modifications that would help.

One owner with both the skills and the materials was Ralph Lee, a Harley Street dentist who lived in Surrey at the time. He decided to move himself, his wife, and daughter into their Cheltenham caravan for the duration of the war. He set about adapting the van to ensure it would stay warm and cosy throughout the cold weather. He installed much-improved insulation and a wood burner, which would keep the van warm and would also heat the water. They then moved the van to Guildford where they pitched in a field. Surviving the war, Ralph later became the first Chairman of The Cheltenham Owners Club, and his daughter married Cecil Gardner.

Cheltenham Crockery included in the purchase price.

THE ELAND (17 ft. 6 in.)

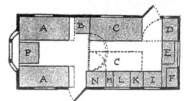

A, A *single beds* ; **B** *coat cupboard* ; **C,C** *single beds* ; **D** *toilet room* ; **E** *wash basin* ; **F** *china cupboard* ; **I** *cooker* ; **K** *store cupboard* ; **L** *sink* ; **M** *writing desk, loose seat* ; **N** *wardrobe* ; **P** *chest of drawers*

Above left: The new shape 1939 Eland with bay window.

Above right: 1939 Eland new floorplan.

Post War – 1955

After the war, with the loss and destruction of many properties, caravans were in high demand. As property was in short supply, owning or renting a caravan was not only a cheaper alternative but a more favourable option than living with relatives or in rooms. Workers rebuilding the country, or anyone who needed to move around from place to place, found them a good alternative to finding rooms to rent in each location they worked. The vans provided a 'Home from Home'.

Many caravan companies did not restart production after the war. However, twenty-five years after originally starting to build caravans, the Cheltenham Caravan Company resumed production. They produced two four-berth models – the once again newly improved Eland, and the Reindeer.

The company still endeavoured to keep ahead of the market, wanting to provide the best caravan in their class and to make it as reasonably priced as possible without compromising on quality. All vans now included double-panelled walls, gas lights, and cookers.

Above left: The 1945 Eland interior rear view.

Above right: The 1945 Eland interior front view.

FOUR BERTH **ELAND**

Left: The 1945 Eland.

Below: The 1945 Eland floorplan.

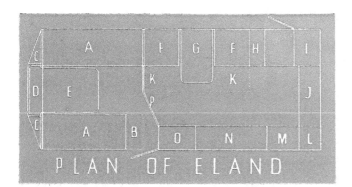

A. Two single beds
B. Extending bed arm
C. Front shelves
D. Ottest heater compartment
E. Detachable table
F. Dinette double beds
G. Detachable table
H. Hanging space
I. Elsan lavatory
J. Wash bowl cabinet
K. Slides forming double bed
L. Calor gas compartment
M. Cooker
N. Writing desk and lockers
O. Wardrobe
P. Dividing doors

Wheeler family with 1945 Reindeer.

Right: 1945 Reindeer.

Below: 1945 Reindeer floorplan.

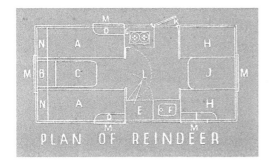

A. Two single beds
B. Ventilated food cupboard
C. Folding table
D. Two roof lockers
E. Wardrobe
F. Washbasin. Draining tray
G. Cooker recess. Airing cupboard. Pan cupboard
H. Dinette seats
I. China locker
J. Folding table
K. Entrance door
L. Folding door
M. Windows
N. Roof lockers

1945 Reindeer interior.

The photograph above is typical of many taken in happy times when the discerning motorist had the car of his choice and chose a CHELTENHAM as the ideal caravan to go with it.

Being one of the earliest and best-known English firms in the industry, we have, during the course of years, received hundreds of letters from satisfied owners all over the world whose testimony has endorsed the fine reputation which CHELTENHAM CARAVANS possess.

CHELTENHAM CARAVAN Co. Ltd.

Registered Office and Works :—

MAIDA VALE WORKS, NAUNTON LANE

CHELTENHAM

Telephone : Cheltenham 3572

Also at 205 Leckhampton Road, Cheltenham

1945 Cheltenham publicity page.

Getting back into production along with high demand for the vans meant that delivery dates were sometimes delayed. The company hoped that the high quality of the vans would make the wait worthwhile.

1948

Around 1948, the post-war 'Gnu' model was produced, using aluminium panelling in place of the pre-war steel body. The first batch of Gnus had a completely separate outside roof, which was insulated against heat and sound. It was suspended about two inches above the inner roof, which allowed air to circulate in between, giving superb ventilation. The roof had to be produced by panel-beaters as it was outside the scope of the skills of the company workforce. Due to the beaters' delays and their escalating costs, only around twenty-five were made with this roof. The later ones had a conventional roof fitted. The rest of the van was insulated between the inner and outer panels with glass fibre insulation material. The model had an Ottest Radiator paraffin heater fitted at the front of the van, in the centre under the window. It was stated that the heater would run for three days and nights on one filling. The model cost £625.

One of the main selling points of the Cheltenham caravans remained the quality and strength of the Cheltenham Chassis. Each chassis was fabricated by the company in their own works. This enabled them to be adapted for each model, ensuring the best pairing was accomplished. They were constructed of angled steel, which had been specially selected; this was braced across with steel angle, making it very strong. The chassis were triple-tested against stress and strains and proved well able to withstand all the adventures it was likely to encounter on its many journeys.

Prior to the war the aluminium arrived by train. Close to the onset of the war one of the expected loads did not arrive and, much to everyone's surprise, it was delivered to the company after the war had ceased. The delivery train wagon had been safely parked up for the duration and remained untouched. Once normal work resumed, it was discovered and delivered to the works.

The
"**Cheltenham**"

FOUR BERTH

G N U

Above left: 1948 Gnu leaflet.

Above right: 1948 Gnu's exterior.

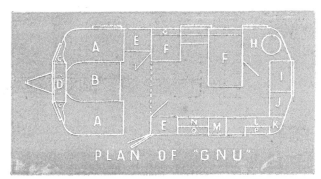

A—Dinette double bed
B – Table
C—Curved shelves

D—Ottest heater below shelf unit
E —Wardrobe
F—Double bed
G   Roof locker and shelves
H—Toilet room
I —Cooker over cupboard
J ⋯Ventilated food cupboard
K⋯Gas cylinder locker
L —Sink and draining board
M—Dressing table with hinged mirror and stool under
N Chest of drawers and locker
O—Bookshelf over chest of drawers
P—China and cutlery cupboard

1948 Gnu floorplan.

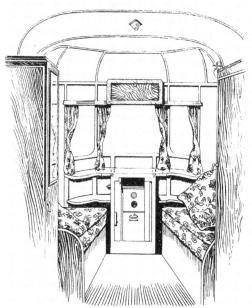

THE 'CHELTENHAM' CHASSIS

The chassis for all "Cheltenham" caravans are designed and fabricated in our own works, thus we are able to meet exactly all the special requirements of each individual mode.

Basically constructed of stout gauge channel steel, braced and cross braced with steel angle or wooden bearers, according to the size of the chassis, they are designed to stand up to the rigours of all forms that a caravan and chassis are likely to meet.

Thick leaf non-rolling springs are employed always, and wherever possible a dropped axle is used, giving a low centre of gravity and exceptional stability when the caravan is in motion. A straight axle is only used when the length of the caravan calls for additional clearance at the extreme ends, and on shorter models for export when exceptional conditions have to be met.

The towing head, specially cast to fit snugly onto the tow-bar vee angle irons, has a coil spring and a shock absorber to eliminate snatching when the caravan is in motion, thus ensuring a smooth tow. It also incorporates an over-run braking system, strong, simple and effective, and safety stirrup.

A built in jockey wheel is supplied as standard on all the models. The hitch is instantly attachable and detachable and a double safety catch is employed.

An instant adjustment on the towing socket collar allows all wear to be taken up, so that towing should always be rattle-free. The single stud ball pin, fitted vertically, ensures that no ugly projection is necessary on the tow bar of the car.

Brace-operated legs are fitted at all four corners, simply and quickly operated without trouble, firmly stabilising the caravan when parked.

Grease nipples are fitted to ensure lubrication for all the moving parts, including the shackle bolts and tow bar.

Easiclean wheels and attractive chromium plated hub caps complete the chassis. Tyres and tubes vary with each model, and are in all instances of a sufficiently large capacity to carry the models with comfort and safety.

Above left: 1948 Gnu interior rear view.

Above right: 1948 Gnu interior front view.

Left: 1945 chassis description.

THE Cheltenham CHASSIS

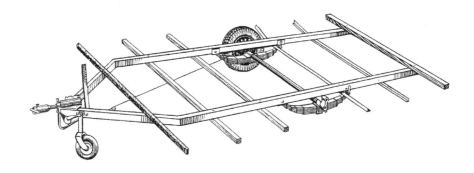

1945 chassis.

1948

In 1947/8, Mr Gardner was ill and needed to relocate to a better climate. He and a Cheltenham distributor decided to move to South Africa and they opened a Cheltenham importing company near Port Elizabeth. Only two vans were imported before the government imposed a huge import tax, to protect local industry. This killed the venture off immediately. Mr Gardner returned home shortly afterwards.

At the Motor Exhibition at Earls Court in 1948, Cheltenham displayed three models; The Eland (£785), The Gnu (£650), and The Reindeer (£460). The Reindeer had been extended to be 6 feet 9 inches wide in order to gain extra floor space. The Eland and the Gnu were said to be 'eminently suitable as a home'.

1950

In 1950, the Gazelle – a 12-foot three-berth model – was tested by *The Caravan* magazine. In the test, the caravan was towed by a Morris Minor. The report stated 'everything possible has been done to ensure perfect behaviour on the road'. They also commented that 'in a relatively small space the owners had produced a van in which one can holiday in real comfort'.

The Cheltenham Owners Club was founded in 1950 after a free rally was organised by the Gardners at their farm for all Cheltenham Owners. (*See separate chapter for more details.*)

During the fifties more people became car owners and petrol was no longer rationed, both of which resulted in caravanning becoming much more widespread.

The Antelope model, which had first been produced in 1938, was reintroduced – a four-berth costing £359. It was lightweight and could be towed by a small sized car. The family van had a centre kitchen and plenty of storage space, and retained the light, airy feel that all Cheltenham caravans have. The van could be split into two sections by opening out the wardrobe door across its width. Being lightweight it was easy to move and, as it did not have a Jockey wheel, a substantial skid in its place which prevented the hitch from dropping and which would take the load when it was standing without steadies.

After conducting a test on the Antelope, *The Motor* magazine stated, 'The good reputation of the makers is undoubtedly justified. The caravan combines unusually comfortable and convenient quarters for its type, coupled with lightness which brings a fair-sized, well-built touring vehicle with four berths, within the practical towing capabilities of a number of motorists who may otherwise be limited to more restricted accommodation through lack of prime mover capacity.'

This year on the way to the FICC Rally in Florence, the Gardners attended a pre-rally meet in Beaune, where they were sited in the town square. They had to buy six-inch nails in order to secure the awnings as they were on asphalt. When the twenty vans were leaving Beaune, they were given a police escort to the Italian border. They were then given an escort all the way to Florence by six motorcycle police officers. One of the officers went

Arthur and Cecil Gardner – Winners of the Brighton Trophy.

ahead and closed the junctions and two followed behind to hurry up the stragglers. The Gardners won the Concours D'Elegance, which was a surprise as they didn't even realise there was a competition taking place.

1952

The 'Deer' model was introduced as a replacement for the pre-war Fawn. The Deer was a barrel-sided model, which was more challenging to produce. In the Deer, the toilet door and wardrobe door could meet across the van, giving a reasonably-sized private area for toilet, washing, and changing. It had a Thames Blue exterior.

Extras included: double-panelled roof of insulation board – £9 10s 0d – and exterior panelling of 18-gauge aluminium alloy – £15 extra.

As the company implemented changes to the design, parts, or layout, it would use up the remaining stock before starting to use the new. This resulted in some improvements starting midway through the year. If a number of improvements or alterations were scheduled for the same year, each one could be implemented at a different time, making some of the vans quite individual. This needs to be taken into account when trying to date the vans today.

The Owners Club Christmas card 1952, featuring Cecil Gardner towing a scaled-down version of a Cheltenham caravan, which had been made as a special request for a customer.

1953

In 1953, for the first time since the war, supplies were easier to come by and the company included the following in that year's sales brochure.

The foreword in the 1953 brochure reads:

The supply position is at last becoming a little easier and we are happy to offer for 1953, a range of models with our usual high quality finish, but better equipped than has been possible since the war.

A word about the perspex "crocks" now being supplied with all models, would not perhaps be out of place. They are light in weight, attractive and very serviceable, being made from genuine Perspex. They should not be confused with certain other plastics, which are a totally different quality.

It is now 32 years since our first caravan was built, just after the 1914-1918 war. As in the past our policy during 1953 will be first and foremost to produce the best possible caravan in its class. Even so, you will find our prices very reasonable.

We are offering all models panelled in Aluminium as an alternative for those who prefer them that way. This does not imply that the standard van panelled, as we do it, in genuine Masonite is inferior. A number of caravans at our own Rally, thus panelled 14 or more years ago, were in excellent condition.

The Perspex crockery was made in the same material as the sinks and was supplied by the same company, which was based in Cirencester.

Brochure, 1953.

The Cheltenham Company had once again increased the range of vans for sale and produced five different models this year; the Deer, Antelope, Bison, Eland and Gazelle.

At this year's 'International Caravan Rally', in Copenhagen, there were, once again, more Cheltenham vans attending in the English section than any other make of van, demonstrating that Cheltenhams were extensively used and preferred by the more experienced and adventurous caravanner. Being lightweight, having excellent towing stability and a well-planned, spacious interior, this made them the perfect caravan for use on long journeys abroad, covering a wide variety of terrains.

This year also saw the first 'Roll on/Roll Off' Ferries introduced between Dover and Calais, which made caravanning in Europe so much easier than previously. This started an upsurge in the numbers of caravan being towed abroad.

Above: New Perspex crockery.

Right: Perspex caravan sink and draining board.

1954

No new models were produced during this year. The company had decided to concentrate on making improvements to the existing models.

The vans were constructed of solid ash frames and the window surrounds were made from hiduminium – high-duty aluminium – which was used extensively in the aircraft industry as it is lightweight and very durable. The models were flat fronted, with the exception of the Eland, which had a bay window at the front. The vans were painted Thames Blue but could be supplied in any colour at extra cost.

The Gazelle, a three-berth caravan, was designed and built as a lightweight model and aimed at people who travelled long distances or to those who had a small car.

The two-berth Deer is a different layout fitted into the same outer shell as the Gazelle.

The Antelope is a lightweight four-berth model. The kitchen is in the middle of the van, over the axle. The V-shaped roof is insulation board covered in specially waterproofed canvas which was painted white. Internally, it had cream walls, a white ceiling, and oak furniture.

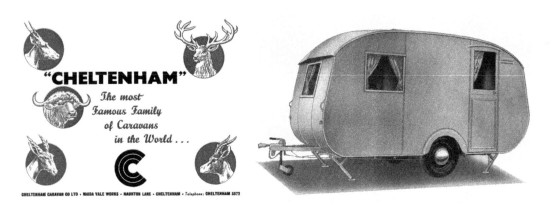

Above left: 1954 Sales brochure.

Above right: 1954 Gazelle and Deer exterior.

A—Single bed. B—Wash bowl. C—Gas hotplate with cupboards and drop flap underneath. D—Food cupboard with china cupboard and shelves above. E—Dinette double bed. F—Detachable table. G—Chest of drawers and gas cylinder cupboard. H—Wardrobe.

1954 Gazelle floorplan.

1954 Gazelle interior.

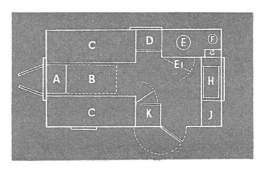

A—Chest of drawers. B—Detachable table. C—Single beds. D—Food cupboard. E—Toilet. F—Gas cylinder stowage position. G—China cabinet. H—Sink and draining board. J—Cooker with airing cupboard above. K—Wardrobe.

1954 Deer floorplan.

1954 Deer showing the double-skin roof.

1954 Antelope.

1954 Antelope interior.

Left: 1954 Bison.

Below: 1954 Bison floorplan.

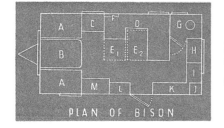

A—Double bed dinette
B—Table   C—Chest of drawers
D—Lounge unit—forming double bed with slides E1 and E2
E1 and E2—Slides completing double bed (The second table also fixes in position E2)
F—Paper rack and mirror (on flap making partition with Compactum doors)

G—Toilet
H—Full cooker and plate rack
I—Ventilated food cupboard
J—China Cabinet
K—Combined sink and draining board lockers under (one for water ca
L—Locker with long drawer for ladi
M—Compactum

38

1954 Bison interior showing the single skin roof.

Above left: 1954 Eland.

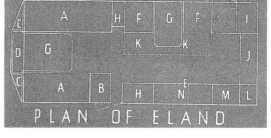

Above right: 1954 Eland floorplan.

PLAN OF ELAND

A—Two single beds (nearside single bed "A" pulls out to position A, B when required full length).   B—Extending bed arm.

C—Front shelves.   D—Chest of drawers.

E—Gas fire.   F—Dinette double bed.

G—Detachable tables.   H—Wardrobes.

I—Elsan lavatory.   J—Washbowl cabinet.

K—Slides forming double bed.

L—Calor Gas compartment accessible through an outside door, and having above on the inside a fitted china cabinet and detachable rubbish tray.

M—Cooker with airing cupboard above.

N—Writing desk, cocktail cabinet, wash hand basin-cum-dressing table, stool, lockers.

1954 Eland floorplan key.

1954 Eland interior.

The four-berth Bison – proved to be a best seller – had a choice of finish for the furniture; either limed or hand-polished oak. It was constructed similarly to the Antelope, with easy manoeuvrability and was an ideal touring van.

The Eland had oak-faced plywood panelling and furniture. It also had a white ceiling with ash roof sticks. The ceiling and walls were insulated with fibreglass, affording triple insulation. The two doors of the wardrobes on either side of the van closed across the middle to create two separate areas. The exterior was sage green with chrome handling rails, louvres, hubcaps, wheel valances, and water pipes, which take the water from the roof to the floor. It had a lantern roof with three opening roof lights on each side. The floor was tongued and grooved with insulation on top, then lino and a carpet runner. There was also a panel gas heater fitted.

The reputation of Cheltenham vans remained excellent and ensured they had a very good resale value, which could be taken into account when considering the purchase price of a new Cheltenham van. All the vans came with a 'Cheltenham Guarantee', which was valid for one year from purchase.

This year's FICC rally was at Innsbruck and all attending Cheltenham owners were invited by the Gardner family to a dinner. This started a tradition that proved to be very enjoyable and which continued at all the FICC rallies, until Mr Gardner died.

There is no information about the Impala other than the list above. It is likely that it would have been in production for a short amount of time.

Guarantee

Our products are guaranteed for a period of one year from delivery. This guarantee is limited to the free replacement of parts which we consider defective in material, workmanship or design and which have been returned to us carriage paid.

This guarantee does not apply to any caravan or parts which have been tampered with or altered in any way and parts not of our manufacture carry the guarantee given by their respective makers.

As our policy is to incorporate improvements immediately they become desirable, our productions may not conform to illustrations, descriptions or drawings published here or elsewhere.

Above left: Equipment list.

Above right: Cheltenham 'Guarantee'.

"CHELTENHAM" CARAVANS

•

1954 PRICES
(EX WORKS)

GAZELLE	- -	£328
DEER	- -	£335
ANTELOPE	-	£379
BISON	- -	£485
ELAND	- -	£795

•

CHELTENHAM CARAVAN CO. LTD
MAIDA VALE WORKS, NAUNTON LANE, CHELTENHAM
TELEPHONE 3572

OPTIONAL EXTRAS ON 'GAZELLE' AND 'DEER'
Aluminium Exterior - £12 10s.   Double panelled roof - £9 10s.
Folding step - £2 5s.

"CHELTENHAM" CARAVANS

•

1955 PRICES
(EX WORKS)

DEER	- - -	£338
ANTELOPE	- -	£385
BISON	- - -	£498
IMPALA	- - -	£650
ELAND	- - -	£815

•

CHELTENHAM CARAVAN CO. LTD
MAIDA VALE WORKS, NAUNTON LANE, CHELTENHAM
TELEPHONE 3572

1954 and 1955 price lists.

1956–63

1956 – Cheltenham: The most famous family of caravans in the world

This year the company advertised new substances, new designs, new features and new layouts, making the 1956 range especially attractive. The Deer was the only surviving model from the previous year. Four new models were introduced to the range: Springbok, Stag, Klipspringer and Sable.

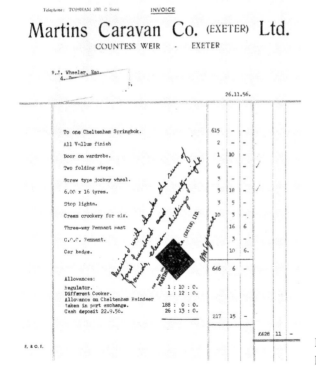

Receipt for 1956 Springbok purchased by the Wheeler family.

The Most Famous Family of Caravans in the World

"CHELTENHAM" CARAVANS
for
1956

NEW

substances, new designs, new features and new layouts make the 1956 'Cheltenham' range specially attractive.

Foremost among them is the 'Springbok' (see front page). This is a bay-front caravan with delightful lines and curves : finished in a special colour scheme of vellum and sky-blue. The body panelling is glass reinforced resin and aluminium. Oak interior, with 1 double and 2 single berths. Two doors. End Kitchen with formica working surfaces. Toilet.

It has a fibre-glass reinforced polyster resin roof, double panelled and embodying the special Cheltenham 'Morlite' glass opening section 6ft. x 4ft., affording unique ventilation and light-giving properties. Curved sides and rounded-corner polished alloy windows, give finishing touches to an elegant appearance. There is a good view through the caravan from the car when on tow.

Furnishings include 4in. latex foam mattresses, special base. Padded back rests. Four cushions, Curtains. Equipped with gas and electric lighting : cooker, regulator, water pump, water carrier, toilet, fitted carpet, paper rack. Table, chest of drawers and bay shelf have heat-resistant finish. Weight (including equipment) ex works is under 17½ cwt. 'Cheltenham' undergear, 5.50 x 16 tyres, 2in. hitch jockey wheel. Price **£595**.

'Cheltenham'
SPRINGBOK
Length 15ft. 8in. Width 6ft. 9in.
4-BERTH End Kitchen & Toilet

A	Single beds	G	China cabinet
A1	Nearside single bed extension	H	Combined sink and draining board and water pump
B	Chest of drawers		
C	Dinette sliding double bed	J	Drawer and locker
D	Toilet	K	Compactum
E	Cooker	L	Detachable Tables
F	Ventilated food cupboard	M	Paper rack and flap for partition

Roof lockers above offside single and double beds. Also above sink unit.

'Cheltenham'
STAG
Length 14ft. Width 6ft. 5in.
4 BERTH End Kitchen and Toilet

This four berth model, with two double beds, and kitchen and toilet, has the distinctive Cheltenham shape, and the new fibre-glass reinforced resin roof with the 'Morlite' section 6ft. x 2ft. Exterior body is panelled with aluminium and the interior with hardboard. Furnishings include deep spring interior mattresses, four cushions and curtains. Equipment includes gas and electric lighting, toilet, regulator, strip carpets, jockey wheel, etc. Undergear as on 'Springbok'. This model has an ex-works weight of 16 cwt. Price **£435**.

A	Dinette double bed	G	Combined sink and draining board
B	Locker	H	Cupboard
C	Settee double bed (C1)	J	Compactum
D	Toilet	K	Detachable table
E	Cooker unit		
F	Food cupboard		

'Cheltenham'
KLIPSPRINGER
14ft. x 6ft. 9in.
2 BERTH & 3 BERTH

A 14ft. De Luxe model having the same bay window front, curved sides, special colour scheme and rounded corner windows that give the 'Springbok' its graceful appearance and beauty of line. Also it has the special 'Morlite' roof.

Exterior body panelling is aluminium and glass-reinforced resin. Oak interior. Alternative lay-out for two or three persons.

Two berth model has two single beds of 6in. Dunlopillo which can be formed into a double bed ; or 4in. Dunlopillo on special base as in the 'Springbok'. Equipment includes two wardrobes, fitted gas fire, second wash basin and padded full backrests, and the items mentioned below.

The three berth model has a single bed dinette and daytime seat across the bay window, and a sliding double bed dinette fitted with 6in. Dunlopillo, in the centre of the offside.

Equipment includes water carrier, water pump, cooker, fitted carpet, toilet, paper rack, etc. Weight 16 cwt. ex works, with undergear as on the 'Springbok'. Price, 3 berth **£565** ; 2 berth **£575**.

A	Single beds	H	Ventilated food cupboard
A1	Single bed extension	J	China cabinet
B	Chest of drawers	K	Combined sink and draining board
C	Wardrobe	L	Compactum
D	Handbasin	M	Detachable table
E	Gas fire		
F	Toilet		
G	Cooker		

And for column 2 (Klipspringer upper legend):

A	Single bed dinette	G	China cabinet
B	Chest of drawers	H	Sink and draining board and lockers
C	Dinette double bed	J	Compactum
D	Toilet	K	Detachable table
E	Cooker		
F	Food cupboard		

'Cheltenham'
DEER
2 BERTH Length 12ft. Width 6ft. 5in.

This very popular 12ft. model is continued and incorporates major improvements. These include exterior body panelling of aluminium and double panelled fibre-glass reinforced resin roof. The interior walls are double panelled with hardboard. Two single berths, with 4in. Dunlopillo mattresses. End kitchen and toilet. Furnished with latex mattresses, cushions, curtains. This model can be supplied with optional layout giving one double or two singles. 'Cheltenham' undergear. Weight ex works 12½ cwt. Price **£355**.

A	Chest of drawers	G	China cabinet
B	Detachable table	H	Sink and draining board
C	Single beds	J	Cooker with airing cupboard above
D	Food cupboard		
E	Toilet	K	Wardrobe

Gas cylinder stowage position is now under nearside bed, instead of as shown at F

'Cheltenham'
SABLE

The 'Sable' is the de-luxe version of the 'Deer' model, having the same layout and dimensions. The elegant 'Springbok' fibreglass bay window front is used, and a similar colour scheme. Among other refinements are rounded corner windows, a window in the toilet, full padded back rests, special bed bases or 6in. Dunlopillo, oak panelled walls, water pump, cover to cooker and point for gas fire. Equipment is similar to the 'Springbok' and the ex works weight is 12½ cwt. Price **£417**.

All 'Cheltenham' Caravans are sold subject to the usual 'Cheltenham' Guarantee and Terms of Business.

★ FULLY INFORMATIVE ILLUSTRATED COLOUR FOLDERS WILL SHORTLY BE AVAILABLE. WRITE FOR COPY STATING WHETHER INTERESTED IN 4 BERTH OR 2 AND 3 BERTH

CHELTENHAM CARAVAN CO. LTD., NAUNTON LANE, CHELTENHAM

Telephone : Cheltenham 3572

1956 Preliminary Sales brochure.

The Sable was to be redesigned within a few years. This included adding another external door and a redesigned kitchen, making it a much improved area for cooking and storage. It was to become the most popular of all the models.

Above and below: The Wheeler family's 1956 Springbok.

The Wheelers' 1956 Springbok at a rally in 1957.

1957

16ft. 4-BERTH

The **S** 'Cheltenham'
SPRINGBOK

"has immediate eye-appeal"
"grace and pace"
"tows beautifully"

For nearly 40 years 'Cheltenham' Caravans have been the choice of the connoisseur and are still chosen by wise caravanners for the good qualities for which they have been famous for so long

THE 4 OTHER 'CHELTENHAM' 1957 MODELS ARE

14FT 4 BERTH *STAG*   12FT 2 BERTH *SABLE*
14FT 3 BERTH *KLIPSPRINGER*   12FT 2 BERTH *DEER*

'Cheltenham' Owners Club RALLY JUNE 14, 15, 16

CHELTENHAM CARAVAN CO. LTD., 205 LECKHAMPTON ROAD, CHELTENHAM   Phone 53695

May 1957   41

1957 advert for Springbok.

The Cheltenham designed towball and hitches are replaced with a Bird & Billington (B&B) hitch, which has a springloaded cup that latches on to the ball automatically.

1956 Owners Rally.

1957 Stag.

1958

By 1958, The Cheltenham Caravan Company were leading the way, using GRP material in the construction of the vans, and having great success using it to enhance the vans' shape and design. From this year, all the vans were produced with GRP front and back panels, a one-piece roof, and aluminium side panels. The single-panelled roof came down over the sides and the gutters were also moulded into it. This ensured that there would be no seams or joins that could leak anywhere on the roof. Not only did this add to the overall appeal and style of the vans, but it made them lighter, and they were able to be more competitive in price.

The first eight-mile section of motorway was opened this year and the national speed limit when towing was 30 mph.

John Yoxall and Ralph Lee decided to fulfil their dream of taking a caravan to the Arctic Circle. John had wanted to try a few years previously, but had been discouraged after hearing about the appalling, near non-existent roads. Now the Cheltenham Caravan Company wanted John to test the Sable model. After having a discussion with Ralph Lee, who had over twenty-five years' caravanning experience, and who owned a Cheltenham Klipspringer, they decided to attempt it together. John towed the Sable with a 6-90 Wolseley, and Ralph towed with a Standard Vanguard II. They were accompanied by their wives, who acted as navigators. The journey took them across from Newcastle to Oslo before they started the long trek to the Arctic Circle. They were pleasantly surprised as to the good condition of some of the roads, which had a tar surface, and quite shocked by the condition of other parts, which was just stone and earth and could barely be classed as a road. On these sections the earth had often been washed away, causing huge potholes and rough surfaces. John reported afterwards that the roads in Norway may have been slow but never dull. Throughout the adventure they encountered sharp gradients and hairpin bends, which the vans coped with without any problems – although on the third day plenty of power was required to get them to the top of a very steep, narrow road that had a very rough surface. They crossed into the Arctic Circle on the sixth morning of the journey.

The return journey proved to be much more of a challenge, with torrential rain affecting the road surfaces. Pot holes of undetermined depths, filled with water, and narrow, very stony roads caused it to be a hazardous journey home. The caravans proved to be every bit as reliable and sturdy as you would hope them to be. On return the tyre pressure was the same as when they had set off and the only problems seemed to be a few panel pins that had been lost and a few screws that had loosened. This was quite remarkable considering the adventure they had experienced and was a great testament to the quality of the Cheltenham Caravans. They were the first caravanners to be awarded 'The Order of Bluenosed Caravanners'.

1959

The first caravan fridge was fitted. The company initially installed Swiss Farner fridges, before quickly changing to an Axim Cara-Frig. These fridges had a malfunction very occasionally, when tipped severely, and needed to be turned upside-down to correct the

'CHELTENHAM' Touring Caravans

...are built for travel, in fact, there are few corners of the world that a 'CHELTENHAM' has not been.

They are really light and capable of being effortlessly ...wed at high speeds or for long distances.

SPRINGBOK with new exterior styling

Left: Mid-1960s advert for Cheltenham Caravans and Axim Fridges.

Below left: Axim Fridge.

Below right: Axim Fridge in Puku.

problem before it could be used again. After encountering many delivery problems, the Cheltenham Caravan Company bought the Axim company, which allowed them to sort out the production delays and to greatly improve the inversion problem. By the middle of the 1960s, and after much work and effort had been invested into the project, Electrolux marketed a fridge that was more reliable and had a much better ignition system. This resulted in the CCC closing the fridge company. When asked if cut-outs from the vans were used to make the fridges, Cecil Gardner denied that any scrap metal was ever used to make the fridges, and said the rumour was completely unfounded.

Independent suspension was fitted to the Springbok models for the first time.

1960

The 'Puku' model was introduced this year at the request of owners who liked the Sable but had expressed an interest in a two-berth model with slightly more space. The Puku was produced in the same size as the Kudu, (14 feet 4 inches) with a very similar internal design as the Sable, including two doors, an extra wardrobe, a drop-down wash basin, a built-in gas fire, and a cupboard with space for a fridge.

The Waterbuck model's fibreglass resin front had a bay window moulded into it and the back had mouldings for the lights.

The ends were curved and the corners were rounded, which not only strengthened the van, but along with the chrome handles at each corner, greatly added to it aesthetically. The Waterbuck was available as a three-berth (£485) or four-berth (£490) model. The three-berth had a wall locker in place of the bunk bed. Three of the beds were over 6 feet long.

The folding step as illustrated is available as an extra on all models

Above: 1960 Puku.

Right: 1960 Puku floorplan.

P U K U

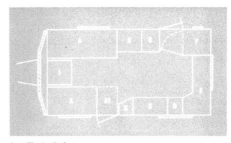

A Single Beds
A1 Floor space in daytime. Bed end moves to form single bed A, A1
B Cocktail/crockery cabinet, with cupboard and fitted gas fire beneath
C Chest of Drawers
D Ventilated food cupboard
E Kitchen unit with griller, combined sink and draining board, pump, with plate rack and cupboards with rubbish bin beneath. Also storage space for gas cylinder and water carriers
B, C, D & E are all working surfaces
F Toilet
G Gentleman's wardrobe with cupboard beneath, ventilated to receive refrigerator if required
H Wide wardrobe
I Chest of drawers, with hinged table on face

49

1960 Puku interior.

1960 Wheeler family celebrating Christmas in the Springbok.

Externally independent springs, which had been used successfully on the Springbok, had been fitted to the Kudu although slightly lighter springs were used.

The four-berth Springbok (£685) retained the large 6 foot x 4 foot 'morlite', which floods the van with light – not always welcome very early on a summer morning, so a roller blind or a venetian blind could be purchased as an extra (approximately £15). The Springbok came with all the equipment the other vans include, plus a fitted carpet and a water carrier. 6.40 x 15 tubeless tyres were standard, although tubed tyres could be supplied.

The world-famous two-berth Sable (£545) stayed unchanged, apart from some minor details, which included a new type of draught excluder and cover moulds.

The models this year had the standard exterior colour Old English White, with Vellum, Pearl Grey, Ice Blue, and Lichen Green also being available. It was possible to have window hoods, gutter mouldings, wheel valances, and the tow-bar shroud highlighted with Carnation Red, Lethbridge Green, Powder Grey, Sky Blue or Thames Blue. Springbok buyers could also request the front and back be painted a different colour from the sides. The vans had a stainless steel waistline trim.

Ralph Lee and his wife took their Cheltenham caravan to the USSR and became the first foreigners to travel through the country unaccompanied by Russian officials.

1961

This year's International Caravan Rally took place in Rome, with a pre-rally taking place in Florence. Arthur and Joy Gardner joined the rally in Rome, meeting up with the other Cheltenham owners and, as had become tradition over the past nine years, they invited the owners to join them for the Cheltenham Owners Club International Annual Party. A large turnout of fifty people attended this year.

1961 Kudu.

Right: 1961 Kudu interior.

Below: 1961 Kudu floorplan.

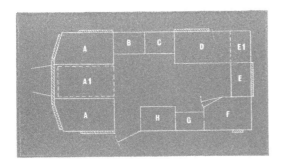

K U D U

A   Double Bed Dinette
A1 Detachable Table also used for forming double Dinette
B   Chest of Drawers
C   Ventilated Cupboard, Wall Cupboard and Book Shelf above
D   Single Bed, Storage Space for Gas Cylinder
E   Cooker Unit with Storage Beneath
E1 Detachable Cover for E—Also Forms working top in Position E1
F   Toilet Compartment
G   Sink and Draining Board with Pump. Storage Space for Water Cans and General Goods Beneath, China Cabinet Above
H   Compactum

1961 Sable.

Left: 1961 Sable interior.

Below: 1961 Sable floorplan.

ERRATA—Stable Door £5.0.0. or glazed Stable Door £7.10.0.

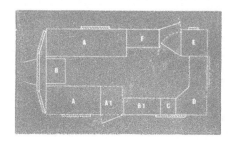

SABLE

A Single beds
A1 Floor space in day time. Bed end moves to
    form single bed A, A1
B,B1 Chests of drawers, with hinged table on face
    of B. Cocktail and china cabinet above B1
C Food cupboard
D Kitchen unit with griller, combined sink and
    draining board, with cupboards underneath
B, C, D are all working surfaces
E Toilet
F Compactum

1961 Springbok.

Right: 1961
Springbok interior.

Below: 1961
Springbok floorplan.

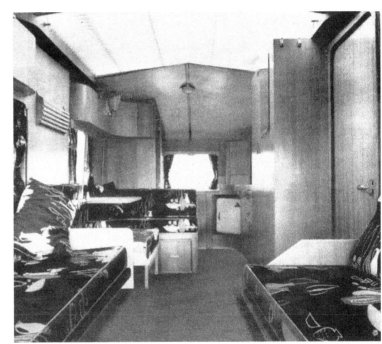

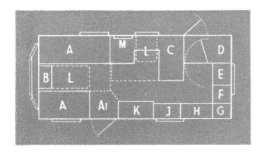

SPRINGBOK

A	Single beds
AI	Nearside single bed extension
B	Chest of drawers
C	Dinette sliding double bed
D	Toilet
E	Cooker
F	Ventilated food cupboard
G	China cabinet
H	Combined sink and draining board and water pump
J	Drawer and locker
K	Compactum
L	Detachable tables
M	Paper rack and flap for partition

Roof lockers above offside single and double beds. Also above sink unit

1961 Waterbuck.

Left: 1961 Waterbuck interior.

Below: 1961 Waterbuck floorplan.

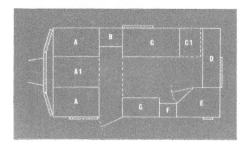

WATERBUCK

A	Double bed dinette seats
A,A1	Double bed using table A1
B	Chest of drawers
C	Single bed
C1	Floor space in daytime. Bed end forms single bed C, C1 at night. Bunk bed above C, C1.
D	Kitchen unit with griller, combined sink and draining board, with lockers beneath and crockery cabinet.
E	Toilet
F	Food cupboard and working surface
G	Compactum. Doors used for dividing caravan into two rooms

"Cheltenham", the finest touring caravan in the world.

Cheltenham Sales Brochure

The models available included Springbok, Puku, Kudu, Sable and Waterbuck. This was the last year the Kudu would be produced. The Puku was also available as a four-berth for the first time. In the four-berth model the front of the van remained the same, but after the door there is a settee that turned into a double bed. The two-berth cost £600 and the four-berth cost £595.

All models had spines moulded into the one-piece roof. The spines improved the strength of the roof and helped to direct the rainwater to the guttering, further eliminating any leakage.

All floors were treated tongued and grooved, which was then covered in insulation felt before the carpet was laid. The vans with aluminium side panels had aluminium foil as cavity insulation, as standard, except for the Waterbuck models, where it was classed as an extra, and could be purchased for £10.

Triumph Herald with Sable.

1962 Roof with moulded spines.

The independent suspension that had been used successfully on the Springbok for the past few years, and the hydraulic shock absorber on the new type head, became standard on all models except the Waterbuck. The shock absorber ensures the brakes are applied smoothly yet powerfully when needed. It has a separate car-type handbrake, which can be applied by the car in the event of a breakaway.

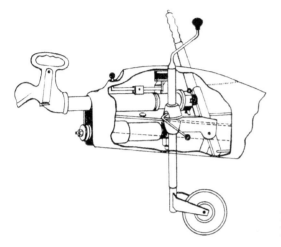

Diagram of shock absorber on new style head.

Gaslight at the front in a Sable.

Gaslight in the kitchen area of a Puku.

EXTRAS
1962 Models

	'SPRINGBOK'	'PUKU'	'KUDU'	'SABLE'	'WATERBUCK'
Glazed Stable Door	£7. 10. 0.	£7. 10. 0.	£7. 10. 0.	£7. 10. 0.	£7. 10. 0.
Stable Door	£5. 0. 0.	£5. 0. 0.	£5. 0. 0.	£5. 0. 0.	£5. 0. 0.
Folding Step	£3. 10. 0.	£3. 10. 0.	£3. 10. 0.	£3. 10. 0.	£3. 10. 0.
Roller Blind	£4. 4. 0.	£4. 4. 0.	£4. 4. 0.	£4. 4. 0.	£4. 4. 0.
Venetian Blind	£15. 0. 0.	£7. 0. 0.	£7. 0. 0.	£7. 0. 0.	£7. 0. 0.
...nier Star Cooker	£7. 10. 0.	£10. 10. 0.	£10. 10. 0.	£10. 10. 0.	£10. 10. 0.
Insulation of walls of "Waterbuck"	standard	standard	standard	standard	£10. 0. 0.
5 pin plug & socket	£1. 4. 0.	£1. 4. 0.	£1. 4. 0.	£1. 4. 0.	£1. 4. 0.
Tip-up wash basin	standard	£9. 0. 0.	£9. 0. 0.	£8. 0. 0.	£8. 0. 0.
Awning Rail	£4. 0. 0.	£4. 0. 0.	£4. 0. 0.	£3. 10. 0.	£3. 10. 0.
Water-pump with flexible lead feed	standard	standard	standard	standard	£4. 4. 0.
Special grade upholstery	£12. 10. 0.	£7. 10. 0. (£12. 10. 0. on 4 berth)	£12. 10. 0.	£7. 10. 0.	£7. 10. 0.
Pennant Mast (3 prong)	£1. 9. 6.	£1. 9. 6.	£1. 9. 6.	£1. 9. 6.	£1. 9. 6.
Refrigerator	£38. 0. 0.	£38. 0. 0.	–	–	–
Hydraulic hitch	standard	standard	standard	standard	£11. 0.
...osquito Nets	£12. 15. 0.	£10. 10. 0.	£11. 5. 0.	£10. 10. 0.	£9. 2. 6.

'Limed' finish }
P.V.C. wall panelling }
Latex foam mattresses }
5" foam on solid base } NO EXTRA CHARGE
for single beds of 'Puku', }
'Springbok' and 'Sable' }
Settee double bed in }
place of single bed & }
bunk in 'Waterbuck' }

Above: Waterbuck with new shroud.

Right: 1962 Price List for extras available with the vans.

Bijou gas lights were fitted to all models and all vans had hand French polished oak walls and furniture. The furniture could be finished in limed oak if desired and the walls panelled in a modern PVC fabric, which was white and incorporated a small buff coloured design. The fabric gave the van a light and much brighter feel and there was also the advantage of being able to wash it down. Externally, the hydraulic coupling was now enclosed in a shroud, making it much neater.

The electric lighting was now fitted with two separate wiring sets. One two-core fed the internals lights and the other, a five-core, fed the external lights, indicators, brakes and so on.

Fifteen per cent of the Cheltenhams ordered this year were ordered with a fridge as an extra (Axim Cara-frig, £38). This was an increase from one-and-a-half percent the previous year. The fridge had a safety cut-off in the event of the flame going out; it did not have a thermostat fitted. Another extra, the shower (£35), was ordered by one-and-a-half per cent, although it was only available for a small number of models.

Cheltenham caravans were increasingly being bought in Ireland.

The Gardners used the FICC rally in Germany to test and show a prototype of the new Fawn. This model was fitted with a door on the offside and had a very large Perspex window at the rear, which slid in guides up to the roof. As this jammed when the van settled down, it was replaced in production with a large window.

1963

The Fawn went into production and was offered for sale. It was the smallest van in the range but, as with all other Cheltenhams, one of the beds was 6 feet 3 inches long, making it comfortable for all.

1963 Springbok.

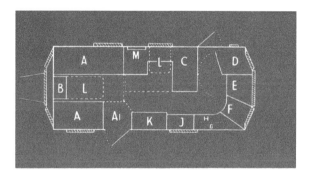

A   Single beds

AI Nearside single bed extension

B   Chest of drawers

C   Dinette sliding double bed

D   Toilet and tip-up wash basin

E   Cooker

F   Ventilated food cupboard or space for refrigerator
     New cutlery drawer

G   China Cabinet

H   Combined sink and draining board and water pump

I   Drawers and locker

K   Compactum

L   Hinged tables

M   Paper rack and flap for partition

Roof lockers above offside single and double beds. Also above sink unit

Book shelf above nearside single bed

1963 Springbok interior.

Springbok had been remodelled. The aluminium back was replaced with a fibreglass rear, which had three bay windows. The front end moulding was revised in style with wrap round front, similar to the rest of the Cheltenham models. The other models still carry on with single window moulded into back GRP wall. All two door models had GRP doors and had an easy clean self-contained moulded GRP toilet compartment. The ceilings on all vans were covered in white PVC.

This year, the legal speed limit when towing was increased to 40 mph.

1964–69

1964

Chassis numbers were revised and now could be used to identify the year, model, and the positon in the production process for that year. The first two digits correspond to the year produced, the next digit relates to the model, and the last two digits are the number in production for that model that year. The production year would start immediately after the summer shut down. 69512 would be the twelfth Sable produced in 1969. 00 would be used on the prototype or show model. Chassis numbers continued to be used in this format when they were later produced by Fernden-Cheltenham Caravan Company Ltd.

The two-inch tow-ball hitch went metric, and was replaced with fifty mm tow-ball.

Travelling abroad was always a major consideration when designing the vans; evidence of this can be seen with the Sable and Waterbuck models, which measure 15 feet 5 inches, including the drawbar. This kept it safely inside the 15 foot 6 inch price range for the cross-channel crossings.

At the FICC rally this year, which was held in Israel – requiring a journey of over 5,000 miles – four Cheltenhams attended, which accounted for half the contingency of

Puku 4 interior.

British caravans. Problems were encountered on the return journey, with some countries not allowing anyone in who had an Israeli stamp on their passports.

1965

Modifications this year included a finned drawbar cover fitted to all models. This would accommodate an electrical reverse lock out, if purchased at extra cost. Tubular vertical grab handles were also fitted to Sables and Pukus.

1966

The 'Nyala' model was introduced during this year, but was only available by special request through Southern Caravans Ltd. It was a four-berth van which, although the same size as the Puku 4, had a completely different layout. The biggest asset must be the bunk beds situated in the bottom corner. This was seen as an improvement on the Puku 4 where the second bed was a double bed, which, when made up, left only a narrow passage, making getting to the facilities rather awkward during the night.

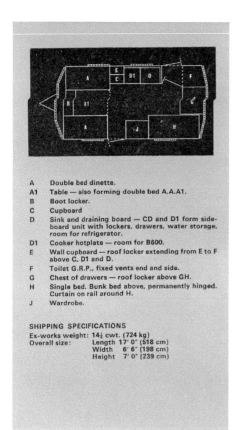

A   Double bed dinette.
A1   Table — also forming double bed A.A.A1.
B   Boot locker.
C   Cupboard
D   Sink and draining board — CD and D1 form side-board unit with lockers, drawers, water storage, room for refrigerator.
D1   Cooker hotplate — room for B600.
E   Wall cupboard — roof locker extending from E to F above C, D1 and D.
F   Toilet G.R.P., fixed vents end and side.
G   Chest of drawers — roof locker above GH.
H   Single bed. Bunk bed above, permanently hinged. Curtain on rail around H.
J   Wardrobe.

SHIPPING SPECIFICATIONS
Ex-works weight: 14½ cwt. (724 kg)
Overall size: Length 17' 0" (518 cm)
           Width   6' 6" (198 cm)
           Height   7' 0" (239 cm)

Left: 1966 Nyala floorplan.

Below: 1966 Nyala.

Above left: Nyala.

Above right: 1966 Nyala interior rear.

All models except the Fawn now have bay windows to the front and rear of the vans, in the same style as previously used in Springboks – enhancing the look of the vans inside and out. It also adds to the storage space at the rear of the vans. Some smaller changes included the internal cupboard handles changing to recessed grey plastic style, and metal door returns.

On 20 July 1966, the Prime Minister decided to decrease the travel-money allowance for British citizens. The limit changed from £250 to £50. This was to impact on those going abroad for more than a week or two. Caravanners needed to plan carefully the routes and mileage they would be travelling, taking into account fuel that would need to be bought. Ever resourceful, they took large stocks of provisions and spent the allowance very carefully, which enabled them to stay away just as long as before. Undeterred, and quite admirably, fifty-six Cheltenham caravans attended the International Rally, which took place this year at Lake Balaton, in Hungary. Once again the Gardner family entertained the rather large contingent of Cheltenham owners at a party evening.

1967

The Springbok was revamped with the revival of the lantern roof – last used over ten years ago. It was now one piece, fully moulded in GRP. This style of roof allowed for an easy ventilation flow as well as making the van more aesthetically pleasing to the eye.

The Fawn caravan had now been in production for four years and was proving to be very successful with those towing on the continent. This model proved to be just as popular today, especially sought after by classic car enthusiasts, those looking for a retro van, and often by those who are caravanning for the first time.

Reacting to feedback regarding the lighting, two of the gas lights have been relocated to become more effective. There are three gas lights in the Springbok and all models also have two electric lights.

To continue to maintain the company's high standards it still ensured that all new models and ideas were tested over the course of three to six weeks and over 3,000 miles

Springboks with new style lantern roof.

1967 Fawn interior.

1967 Fawn interior kitchen.

Fawn with classic car.

before being put into production. The company also continued to offer a free service on all new caravans. The service was available either after two months or after towing for 500 miles whichever occurs first. Included in the service were checks on brakes, chassis, gas and electric lights as well as cupboard catches and retainers.

Cheltenham are still able to produce what is considered in many quarters to be the most comfortable and workable van on the market.

The Caravan, July 1967

1968 Waterbuck.

1968 Waterbuck front.

1968 Waterbuck rear.

Above left: 1968 Waterbuck interior front.

Above right: 1968 Waterbuck interior drawers and cupboard.

Above left: 1968 Waterbuck interior LHS.

Above right: 1968 Waterbuck interior RHS.

1968

GRP glazed stable doors were now offered as an extra on late models. Most buyers took this option for the main door, although a few took the option on the rear door, having opaque glass fitted.

The Fawn GRP roof moulding now ended just below the roof line as with other models. The sides were all aluminium without the seams above the window.

Awning rails were now fitted on all models. The Springbok and Fawn went all the way around.

Mr Gardner passed away in June this year and his son Cecil, who already had a major role in the company, took over the business. The family insisted that the Cheltenham Owners rally still went ahead as planned.

Above left: 1967 Fawn with seam above window.

Above right: 1968 Fawn without seam above window.

Model		Springbok	Nyala Roebuck Puku 2	Sable Waterbuck	Fawn
Body length		16'6" (503 cm)	15'0" (457 cm)	13'4" (406 cm)	11'2" (340 cm)
Shipping Size	Length Width Height	18'7" (566 cm) 6'9" (206 cm) 8'1" (246 cm)	17'0" (518 cm) 6'6" (198 cm) 7'10" (239 cm)	15'5" (470 cm) 6'6" (198 cm) 7'10" (239 cm)	13'4" (406 cm) 6'3" (191 cm) 7'8" (234 cm)
Approx. weight (Ex-works)		17¾ cwt. (902 kg)	14½ cwt. (737 kg)	12¾ cwt. (648 kg)	11 cwt. (559 kg)
Max. all up weight		21¾ cwt.	18 cwt.	15¾ cwt.	14 cwt.
Wheel track		70½"	68½"	68½"	65½"
Tyre size		6.70 x 13 6 ply	6.40 x 13	5.90 x 13	5.60 x 13
Suggested tyre pressure		38lbs. sq. ins.	35lbs. sq. ins.	35lbs. sq. ins.	35lbs. sq. ins.
Hitch height to centre of ball		18"	18"	17½"	17½"

Specifications of 1968 models.

The Springbok saw the most changes this year. The roof-light canopies were no longer being moulded in with the roof; they were now made from separate aluminium pressings. All the drawers were now made from plywood instead of solid oak, which was in line with the other models, and it now had curved end grab handles.

Other changes taking place this year included replacing the window internal surrounds from aluminium to white plastic, and the door thresholds became a smooth folded piece instead of the ribbed version.

The style of the cupboard handles changed to a projecting grey plastic fitting and the Formica tops in all models changed to a cross hatch design.

Advert for Cheltenhams.

Springbok interior which has been restored.

	SPRINGBOK	PUKU	NYALA	SABLE	WATERBUCK	FAWN
Recommended ex works price	£940.0.0.	2 berth £798.0.0. 4 berth £748.0.0.	£748.0.0.	£705.0.0.	£676.0.0.	£584.0.0.

THESE CHARGES APPLY WHEN THE RESPECTIVE ITEMS ARE ORIGINALLY SPECIFIED BEFORE PRODUCTION

EXTRAS

	SPRINGBOK	PUKU	NYALA	SABLE	WATERBUCK	FAWN
Electric Reversing Catch	£8. 0. 0.	£8. 0. 0.	£8. 0. 0.	£8. 0. 0.	£8. 0. 0.	£8. 0. 0.
Glazed Stable Door	£5. 0. 0.	£5. 0. 0.	£5. 0. 0.	£5. 0. 0.	£5. 0. 0.	£5. 0. 0.
Glazed Stable Door on offside	£8. 0. 0.	£8. 0. 0.	£8. 0. 0.	£8. 0. 0.	--	--
Folding Step	£4.10. 0.	£4.10. 0.	£4.10. 0.	£4.10. 0.	£4.10. 0.	£4.10. 0.
Calor B600 Cooker	£12.10.0.	£12.10.0.	£12.10.0.	£12.10.0.	£12.10.0.	--
Pennant Mast (3 prong)	£1.12. 6.	£1.12. 6.	£1.12. 6.	£1.12. 6.	£1.12. 6.	£1. 0. 0.
Refrigerator	£42.12.0.	£42.12.0.	£34.10.0.	£42.12.0.	£34.10.0.	--
Cli-Pon Insect Screens:- a) 2 side windows and rooflight	--	£9.18. 6.	£9.18. 6.	£9.18. 6.	£9.18. 6.	£9.18. 6.
b) Rooflight only	--	£4. 1. 0.	£4. 1. 0.	£4. 1. 0.	£4. 1. 0.	£4. 1. 0.
c) All opening windows	£21.0. 0. (Excluding lantern roof windows)	£18.6. 3.	£21.5. 0.	£18.6. 3.	£15.7. 6.	£16.5.0.
d) All opening windows and rooflight	£21.0. 0.	£22.7. 3.	£25.6. 0.	£22.7. 3.	£19.8. 6.	£20. 6.0.
12 volt Fluorescent Lights	£13.0. 0.	£13.0. 0.	£13.0. 0.	£13.0. 0.	£13.0. 0.	£6.10.0.

NO EXTRA CHARGE FOR THE FOLLOWING:

"Limed" Finish. P.V.C. Wall Panelling. 5" Foam on solid base for single beds of Puku, Springbok and Sable. Settee Double Bed in place of single bed and bunk in Waterbuck. Settee Double bed in place of Double Dinette in Springbok.

Price list for 1969.

1970–77 – Changing Times

The latest model to be added to the range was a Roebuck, replacing the Puku 4. The four-berth van included two single beds at the front of the van, which could be made into a double bed, and a single bed at the rear with a hinged bunk above. The sink and cooker area was in the centre offside of the van, with a food cupboard and space for a fridge at the rear.

The Fawn model was redesigned and now had the door on the nearside. The flooring was tongued and grooved softwood.

1970 Roebuck.

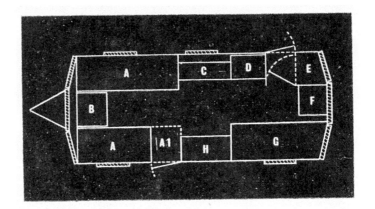

Right: 1970
Roebuck floorplan.

Below: 1970
Roebuck key to
floorplan.

A   Single beds.

A1   Floor Space in day time. Bed end moves to form single bed A, A1.

B   Chest of drawers with hinged extending table on face.

C   Combined sink and draining board. Storage below.

D   Cooker recess with storage below. China cabinet roof locker extends above kitchen units C and D.

E   Toilet compartment G.R.P. with fixed vents.

F   Food cupboard or space for refrigerator.

G   Single bed with hinged bunk above and hinged backrest.

H   Compactum.

		SHIPPING SPECIFICATIONS	
Length	15′ 0″ (457 cm)		
Width	6′ 6″ (198 cm)	Length	17′ 0″ (518 cm)
Headroom	6′ 3″ (191 cm)	Width	6′ 6″ (198 cm)
		Height	7′ 10″ (239 cm)
		Ex-works weight 14½ cwt. (737 kg)	

1970 Roebuck interior.

The Roebuck model was dropped part way through the year.

The Sable and Puku had the drawers, below the china cabinet, replaced with two cupboards.

The rear body mouldings were altered to accommodate the new-style Hella rear lights.

Left: Drawers under the china cabinet (Old style).

Right: Cupboards below the china cabinet (New Style).

Small changes took place this year, including changing the stainless-steel waistband trim to a version that included a black rubber strip through the middle of the band and, internally, the ceiling strips that cover the joints were changed from wood to white plastic.

This year the company took the brave decision to manufacture a less-expensive range of caravans. The 'Explorer' range was produced and aimed at the wider masses of caravan owners. There were to be three sizes of vans: 10-foot, 12-foot and 14-foot. The vans had a B&B chassis in place of the Cheltenham chassis. The sides were flat, not bowed, and were simpler in shape; lacking the style and appeal of the other models, although the new shape provided plenty of head room even into the corners. There is an amber sky light fitted.

The framework of the van was one-and-a-quarter inch, and the wall cavities and the floor were insulated. The layout included a dinette at the rear of the van, which became a double bed at night. When an extension was used, the two settees at the front of the van became two single beds. There was also a bunk which ran across the window approximately eighteen inches above the foot of the two beds. This was easily stored away during the day. The kitchen was positioned in the middle offside of the van, containing a sink and drainer, a Flavel two-ring burner and grill, a Splintex Carastor unit positioned behind one of the doors, and ample storage. The top that covered the sink and drainer formed an extra preparation area when opened.

Explorer model.

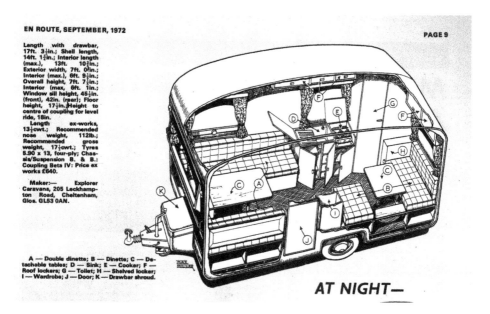

Length with drawbar, 17ft. 3½in.; Shell length, 14ft. 1¾in.; Interior length (max.), 13ft. 10½in.; Exterior width, 7ft. 0½in.; Interior (max.), 6ft. 9½in.; Overall height, 7ft. 7½in.; Interior (max, 6ft. 1in.; Window sill height, 45½in. (front), 42in. (rear); Floor height, 17½in.; Height to centre of coupling for level ride, 18in.

Length ex-works, 13½cwt.; Recommended nose weight, 112lb.; Recommended gross weight, 17½cwt.; Tyres 5.90 x 13, four-ply; Chassis/Suspension B. & B.: Coupling Beta IV: Price ex works £640.

Maker:— Explorer Caravans, 205 Leckhampton Road, Cheltenham, Glos. GL53 0AN.

A — Double dinette; B — Dinette; C — Detachable tables; D — Sink; E — Cooker; F — Roof lockers; G — Toilet; H — Shelved locker; I — Wardrobe; J — Door; K — Drawbar shroud.

AT NIGHT—

Explorer interior.

When tested the van was said to have the same excellent road handling as the established Cheltenham caravans. Unfortunately, the vans were not a success and very few were ever made.

Law came into force this year prohibiting people from being carried in the caravan.

1973 – The 'Modernised' Vans

After the failure of the Explorer range, it was changing times for the original Cheltenham caravans. The furniture was now plywood with photo-etched veneer. Hardwood mouldings were reintroduced to cover the joins on the wall panels. The chipboard flooring that had been introduced previously was once again replaced with tongued and grooved flooring and the underfloor insulation was improved. To comply with regulations, an exterior door was fitted to give access to the gas bottles, and vents were added to the main door and toilet area. Rectangular aluminium handles were fitted to the external doors and, internally, black cupboard handles were now fitted. Die-cast model name badges were fitted to the side of the vans. All vans were finished in Dover White as standard, with other colours available such as Vellum, Pearl Grey, Fiesta Yellow, and Ice Blue. The trims could be painted in any of the above or in Carnation Red, Thames Blue, Powder Grey, or Sky Blue.

The newest addition to the model range was an 'Oribi'. It was a four-berth model and replaced the Nyala. It had the two single beds at the front, which could be altered to make a double, and the centre single bed had a new-design hinged back, which converted easily to become the fourth bed at night. The van could be divided by a curtain at night or a track fitted around the bunks.

A B&B Beta 4 hydraulic over run coupling was now fitted as standard on all models.

1973 Oribi.

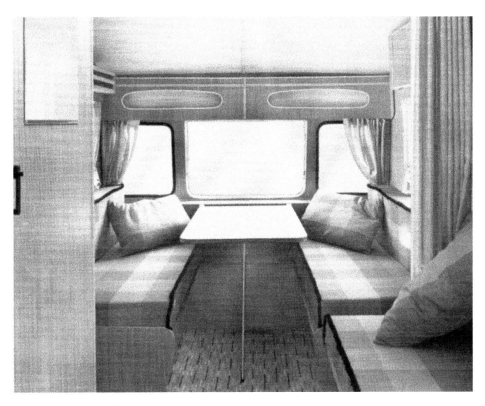

1973 Oribi interior front.

	SPRINGBOK	PUKU 2	ORIBI	SABLE	WATERBUCK	FAWN
Recommended ex works price	£1,528.00	£1,055.00	£988.00	£939.00	£876.00	£768.00

- -

THESE CHARGES APPLY WHEN THE RESPECTIVE ITEMS ARE ORIGINALLY SPECIFIED BEFORE PRODUCTION.

EXTRAS

	SPRINGBOK	PUKU 2	ORIBI	SABLE	WATERBUCK	FAWN
Electric Reversing Catch.	£12.00	£12.00	£12.00	£12.00	£12.00	£12.00
Glazed stable door.	£6.50	£6.50	£6.50	£6.50	£6.50	£6.50
Glazed stable door offside.	---	£9.00	£9.00	£9.00	---	---
Folding steps	£7.00	£7.00 N/s only	£7.00	£7.00	£7.00	£7.00
Calor B600 cooker.	---	£18.50	£18.50	£18.50	£18.50	£18.50
Refrigerator	£56.11	£56.11	£56.11	£56.11	£45.50	£45.50
Cli-Pon Insect Screens: a) 2 Side windows and rooflight	---	£14.34	£14.34	£14.34	£14.34	£14.34
b) Rooflight only	---	£6.00	£6.00	£6.00	£6.00	£6.00
c) All opening windows, excluding lantern roof windows and rooflights.	£28.80	£25.57	£28.98	£25.57	£22.08	£23.10
d) Ditto but including rooflight.	---	£31.57	£34.98	£31.57	£28.08	£29.10
Spring base bed tops	---	£15.00	---	£15.00	---	£15.00
Conversion kit for 2 single beds to double bed.	---	£7.00	---	£7.00	---	£7.00
Extra gas light No. 1 Morco.		£9.00	£9.00	£9.00	£9.00	£9.00

NO EXTRA CHARGE FOR THE FOLLOWING:

5" foam on solid base for single beds of Springbok. Settee double bed in place of single bed and bunk in Waterbuck. Settee double beds in place of double dinette in Springbok.

Price List for 1973 caravans.

1973 Oribi interior rear.

1974

The 'Super Sable' was introduced, being a superior model of the most popular of vans. The Super refers to the added extras that were included as standard. These included an oven, fridge, flued heater, folding step, and glazed stable door. It was built on a heavier chassis than the standard Sable and was easily identified by the double stainless steel waistband trim.

The B&B sigma auto reverse hitch was fitted to all vans and PVC wall cladding became available as an optional extra.

The Government deemed caravans a luxury item this year and consequently the purchase tax increased, adding a substantial amount to the purchase price. The price of petrol had escalated and it was in short supply. The country was deep in a recession. These events, along with a downturn in sales over the last few years, resulted in the family deciding to end production and to close the company.

1974 Super Sable.

1974 Super Sable, minus the folding step.

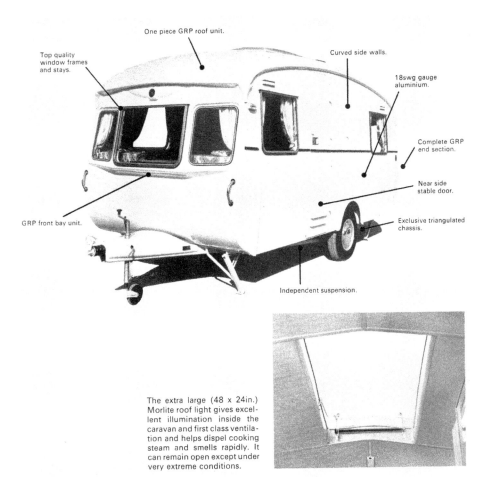

One piece GRP roof unit.

Top quality
window frames
and stays.

Curved side walls.

18swg gauge
aluminium.

Complete GRP
end section.

Near side
stable door.

GRP front bay unit.

Exclusive triangulated
chassis.

Independent suspension.

The extra large (48 x 24in.)
Morlite roof light gives excellent illumination inside the
caravan and first class ventilation and helps dispel cooking
steam and smells rapidly. It
can remain open except under
very extreme conditions.

Practical features of Cheltenham Caravans.

1975

After the company ceased trading, Mrs Gardner and Cecil Gardner agreed to continue fulfilling their roles in the Cheltenham Owners Club.

1976

Stevens & West, parent company of Stirling Caravans, bought Cheltenham Caravan Company Ltd and advertised the Fawn, Sable and Puku models, but they never actually went into production.

The Owners Club newsletter announced that Fernden Caravans of Frant, Kent, have acquired the manufacturing rights for Cheltenham Caravans. It also stated that spares and servicing were available for all existing owners and that they were intending to build a range of four models to special order.

1978–82 – Fernden-Cheltenham Caravans Ltd

In 1978, production began at Fernden Caravans under the supervision of Roger Lander, who had been the production manager at Cheltenham Caravan Company. Although the intention had been to produce four models, they concentrated on two; the Sable and Puku 2. The Sable had been the most popular van for many years. As the reputation of Cheltenham caravans had declined slightly before they ceased trading, the task was now to regain the excellent reputation. They used quality materials and techniques, excellent workmanship, and ensured that attention to detail was in place.

The sales brochures advertise The New Cheltenham Sable and The New Cheltenham Puku 2, by Fernden-Cheltenham Caravans Ltd.

The layout of the vans was kept very much as they had been previously, although the Sable lost some wardrobe space in order for a shower to be incorporated into the washroom. The Sable also had a flued space heater fitted, while the Puku 2 had a central heating system. The system's boiler also supplied the hot water for the sink and the shower system, and was located externally in the gas-bottle locker on the extended A frame. Currently, very few of the vans still have this system in working order. Although parts can still be sourced, most systems have been replaced with a modern heating system. The vans had ceiling mounted fluorescent lights, two reading lights, and one gas light. Items that had been an extra previously now became standard, i.e. a folding step, an Electrolux fridge, and Flavel Oven.

The vans were built with a heavier, more robust framework and chassis, and the brakes allowed reversing to take place without the need for a separate reverse lock. Toughened glass was used for the windows in order to comply with Health and Safety regulations.

In 1979, the windows had drop down vents and were in anodized frames.

In 1980, corner steady legs changed to standard B&B type – splayed out, not in, as Cheltenham style had been.

In 1982 all production ended, with no more Cheltenham Caravans being made.

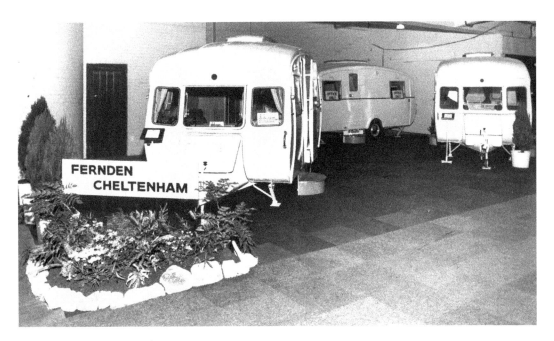

Fernden show stand.

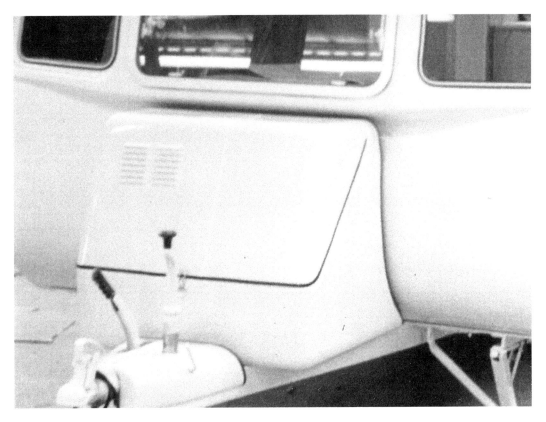

Fernden gas locker.

Working on Fernden vans.

Fernden Puku with new-style windows.

1981: One of the last vans to be made – Fernden Puku interior.

Above and below: Cheltenham caravans towed by classic cars.

Cheltenham caravans towed by classic cars.

The Cheltenham Owners Club

Arthur Gardner enjoyed attending many car club events; meeting up with different people that shared the same interest. He realised that Cheltenham owners may appreciate the opportunity for them to get together. After buying a farm in 1949, Arthur Gardner discussed with his family the idea of holding a rally with the hope of forming a club for Cheltenham owners. It would be somewhere that owners could come together and share friendship and enjoy a social weekend.

The Gardners set about spreading the word about the free rally, which was to be held in early September at their farm. Adverts were placed in caravan magazines, flyers were displayed at showrooms, and the word was spread at other meets and rallies. As with most things that Arthur was involved in, the date had been carefully selected so it did not clash with any of the main summer rallies that took place, but also so that it did not occur too late in the season.

That August had seen more than double the average amount of rain fall, but that did not deter fifty-five vans from attending the rally, although Cecil Gardner – using his new Land Rover Series 1 – had to tow most of the vans on to and off the field. The vans ranged from early 1930s Gazelles, to the newly purchased Elands. Three owners had purchased their vans new more than fifteen years previous and three caravans had been towed on the continent; this number was to increase considerably over the next few years. A gift of a paper knife, inscribed with 'Cheltenham 1950', was given to each van.

During the weekend the Gardner family, never ones to rest on their laurels, took the opportunity to look around the vans to see what improvements or additions people had made, and to talk informally to the owners about what they liked or least liked about the vans. This gave owners the opportunity to give suggestions for future vans.

On the Saturday evening the Gardner family hosted a formal dinner in a marque on the field. The Mayor of Cheltenham and local MPs were among the invited guests. After dinner, it was proposed that 'The Cheltenham Owners Club' be formed. A committee was elected, with Arthur Gardner accepting the role of President. Ralph Lee was elected as Chairman, Cecil Gardner as Secretary, Joy Gardner as Treasurer, and the rest of the committee were also elected. All future events would be organised by the Cheltenham Owners Club committee and helpers. The Gardners offered the use of Southfield Manor Farm for the

Right: Owners Club badge.

Below: Early Owners Club rally at Southfield Farm.

yearly rally. The newly elected committee decided the next Cheltenham Rally would take place in June the following year – 1951.

Over the course of the weekend the members had the option to travel to the factory and have a look around to see how the caravans were made. The family were overwhelmed by the number wanting to take the tour; Mr Gardner and Cecil had a hard task coping with the queue of fifty cars that arrived. The following years they enlisted five employees to help.

The rally had proved to be a great success, although they were very pleased to have a committee to organise future rallies.

In 1964 the committee and members decided to hold two rallies a year. This second rally was to become the 'Northern' or 'Late Summer' rally. It was also proposed that an Irish division of the owners club be formed.

In 1966, the Owners Club had around 1,500 members, and 188 vans attended the Cheltenham Rally at Southfield farm. The highlight of the weekend was, as always, the formal dinner, where distinguished guests joined the family and members for an evening of food and dancing. After dinner, presentations took place. One of the presentations was the 'President's Cup', which was, and still is, presented to the owner who has towed the highest mileage since the previous Cheltenham Rally. This year Miss E. A. Bailey accepted the cup; her towing mileage recorded as 8,984 miles.

Owners Club rally, 1950s, at Southfield Farm.

The bringing together of owners had resulted in many more Cheltenham caravans being towed abroad, especially to the International Caravan Rallies. This year fifty-six Cheltenham caravans attended the International Caravan Rally in Hungary.

The Owners Club was one of the first one marque caravan clubs to be formed and is certainly the oldest surviving today. The club celebrated 65 years in existence in 2015 at the main Cheltenham Rally and is now preparing for its 70th anniversary in 2020. The camaraderie and friendship at events are as evident today as it was in the beginning.

The Owners Club still meet up formally three times a year. The main rally is around Spring Bank Holiday and remains close to the centre of the country, to allow as many members to attend as possible. There is a 'Late Summer' rally in August, which changes venue each year, and a 'Winter Luncheon' takes place in February. There are also informal meets, which members organise – one in Scotland and one in Dulverton.

As the vans get older it is inevitable that they need care and attention if they are to continue to survive. There is a wealth of knowledge in the club gained over many years, which is willingly shared amongst members.

It is certain that Mr Arthur Gardner would be very proud to see so many of the vans in extremely good condition and being in regular use today.

Owners Club rally, 1950s, at Southfield Farm.

Above and below: Owners Club rally, 1960s, at Southfield Farm.

Owners Club rally, 1960s, at Southfield Farm.

Owners Club Christmas card, 1968, Nr. Dobbiaco, Italian Dolomites. Winner of the photography competition – A. G. Barton.

Rally, Harbury.

Owners Club Christmas Card, 1969, Glenshiel – Winner of the photography competition H. R. Broadhurst.

Owners Club Rally.

Owners Club Rally.

Overlooking the Owners Club Rally at Coniston.

Owners Club Rally at Ledbury.

Owners Club Rally 2016 at Harbury Rugby Club, Leamington Spa.

Owners Club Northern Rally 2012 at Christleton, Chester.

Sable showing stable door.

A 'Pot of Gold'.

Further information is available at the Owners Club website – www.cheltenhamownersclub.co.uk

Acknowledgments

My dear husband Tim for his patience, help, and support.

Cecil Gardner, Richard Wheeler and family, John and Jenny Marsland, and Cheltenham
members for all their help and support.